AN AUTHENTIC ADVENTURE

with a Marco Island Burrowing Owl

Melissa Waters

⭐ **A zillion extra special thanks to the stars of the story!** ⭐
Fran Erickson
Brittany Piersma
Sharon Epple
Burrowing Owls of Marco Island – facebook.com/OwlWatchFL
Audubon Western Everglades – audubonwe.org
Marco Island Brewery – marcoislandbrewery.com
Island Time – facebook.com/IslandTimeMarcoIsland
The Crazy Flamingo – thecrazyflamingo.com
Marco Island Authentics – facebook.com/MarcoIslandAuthentics

...and many thanks to my totally awesome publisher!
Joanne Tailele – simonpublishingllc.com

Published by Simon Publishing LLC

Cover & Interior Design by Melissa Waters

Photo Credits

JÉSHOOTS https://www.pexels.com/@jeshoots/
p. 1 – https://www.pexels.com/photo/apple-communication-digital-iphone-3605/
p. 2 – https://www.pexels.com/photo/apple-hand-iphone-mobile-phone-3627/

Eileen Pickett Kivlin – p. 17

Burrowing Owls of Marco Island – pp. 8, 19 and 20

Adobe Inc – Adobe Illustrator – p. 20 https://adobe.com/products/illustrator

Microsoft PowerPoint – microsoft.com/en-us/microsoft-365/powerpoint Gallery theme

Melissa Waters – all photos not cited above

ISBN: 979-8-988 2937-8-1 (Paperback)
ISBN: 979-8-988 2937-9-8 (Hardcover)
ISBN: 979-8-989 4345-4-1 (eBook)

Library of Congress Control Number: 2023921290

DEDICATION

To my wonderful parents, Carolyn and Maurice Sherman, who introduced me to Marco Island and its beautiful burrowing owls.

To my uncle P.J. Lamb, who inspired me to write this book, and my aunt Pamela Lamb, who helped me edit my draft.

And to my beautiful daughters, Casey Cordova and Danielle Rosa, and my awesome grandchildren, Xander Boivin, Addy Cordova and Wyatt Cordova.

❤ **I love you all** ❤

AN AUTHENTIC ADVENTURE

---

with a Marco Island Burrowing Owl

Simon Publishing, LLC

Once upon a time, as I sat down for dinner at the **Marco Island Brewery...**

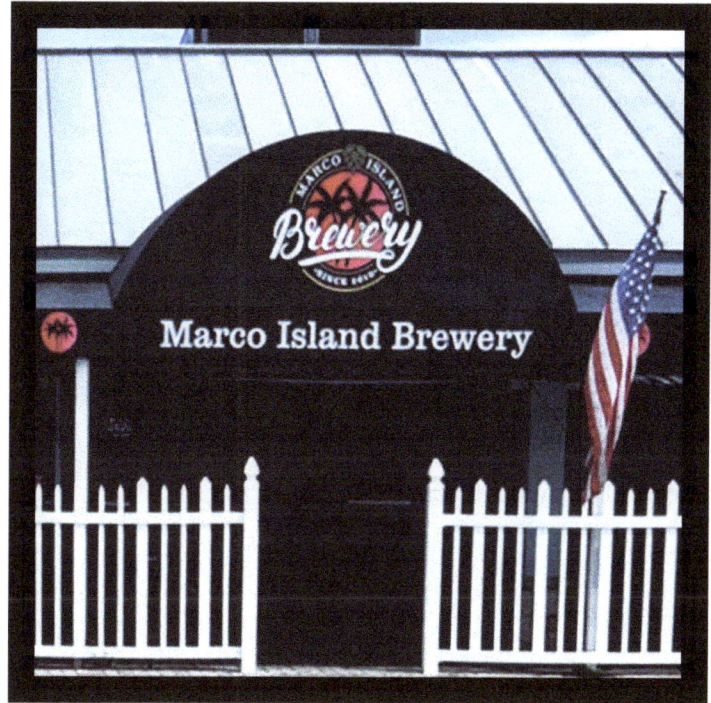

...a lady came to my table with a cell phone in her hand.

She pointed to the picture on her phone and said, "Hi, I'm Fran. This beautiful owl is sitting outside my shop. Come, let me show you!"

I said, "Hi, Fran, I'm Melissa. I'd love to see the owl" and I followed her toward her shop, **Marco Island Authentics**.

Sure enough, an adorable little **burrowing owl** stood in the parking lot outside the shop's door.

I said *"Oh, how cute!"* as I admired the little owl.

Some shoppers stopped and joined us to take pictures.

I took a few pictures, thanked Fran, and went back to my table.

A short while later, Fran came back and said that the owl was still standing in front of her store.

We both found it strange for a burrowing owl to stay in a busy shopping center for such a long time.

I looked at the pictures on my phone and noticed that the owl's eyes looked very sleepy.

The owl also looked much rounder than most burrowing owls do.

6

Fran worried, "*Maybe the owl is sick!*"

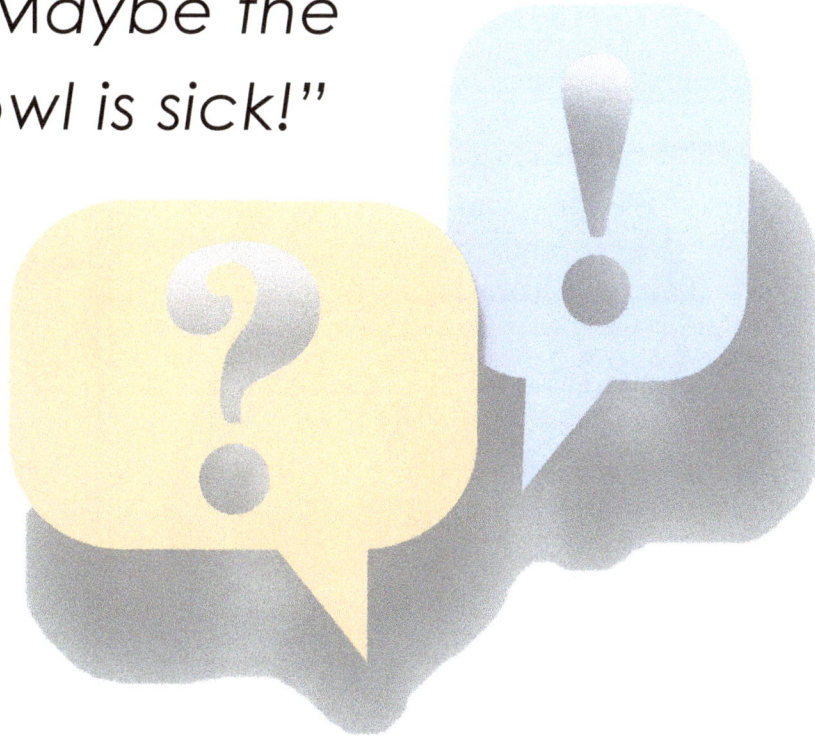

I wondered, "*Maybe it's a mama owl who can't fly back to her burrow to lay her eggs?*"

We agreed to call for help.
I sent a text to the
Marco Island Owl Watch.

Fran made a phone call to
Audubon Western Everglades.

Brittany Piersma, Marco Island Field Biologist, texted, *"Clap your hands near the owl to see if it will fly away."*

I clapped my hands. The owl flew a short distance and landed on one foot.

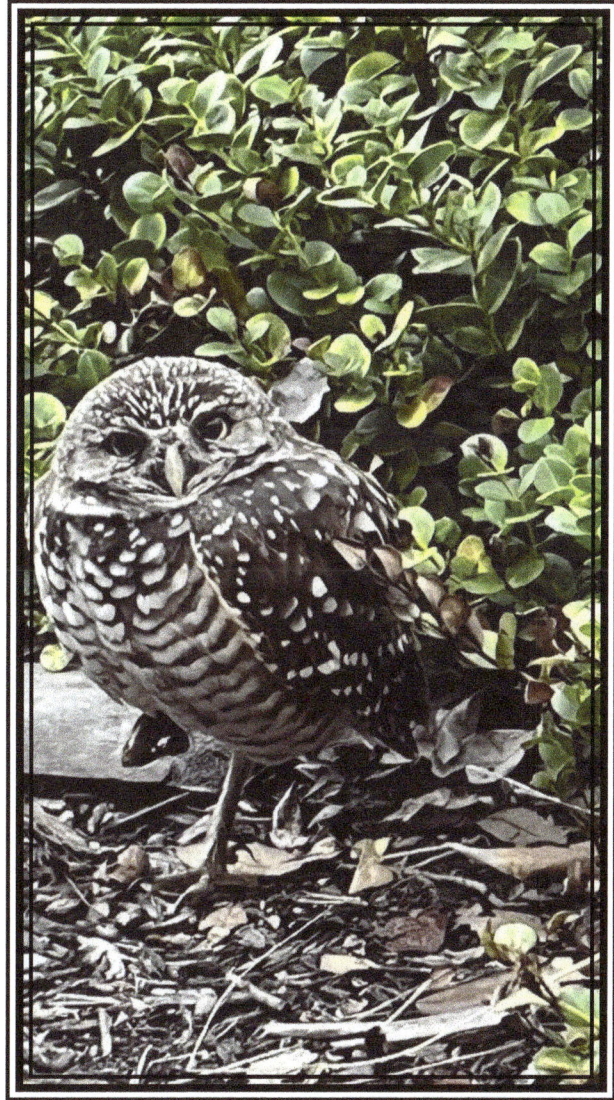

"Oh, no!" I texted back. *"I think the owl has a broken leg."*

Brittany then called me and said "the owl's leg is probably fine. It's normal for an owl to stand on one foot."

As if the owl understood what Brittany had said, it hopped to the side and landed on both feet.

Meanwhile, Fran was on the phone with Sharon Epple, an Owl Watch volunteer.

Sharon asked Fran to catch the owl until she and Brittany could come to the store.

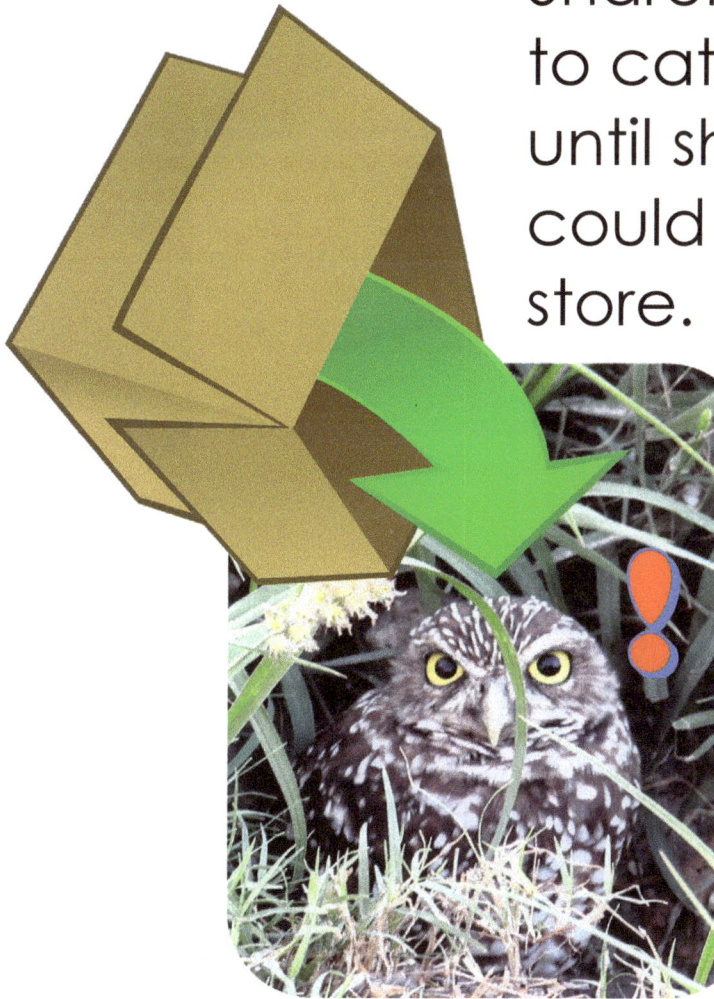

So, we tried to catch the owl with a box!

When we first tried to catch the owl, the owl flew under a truck!

But when we shooed the owl out from under the truck...

the owl flew right back into the bushes.

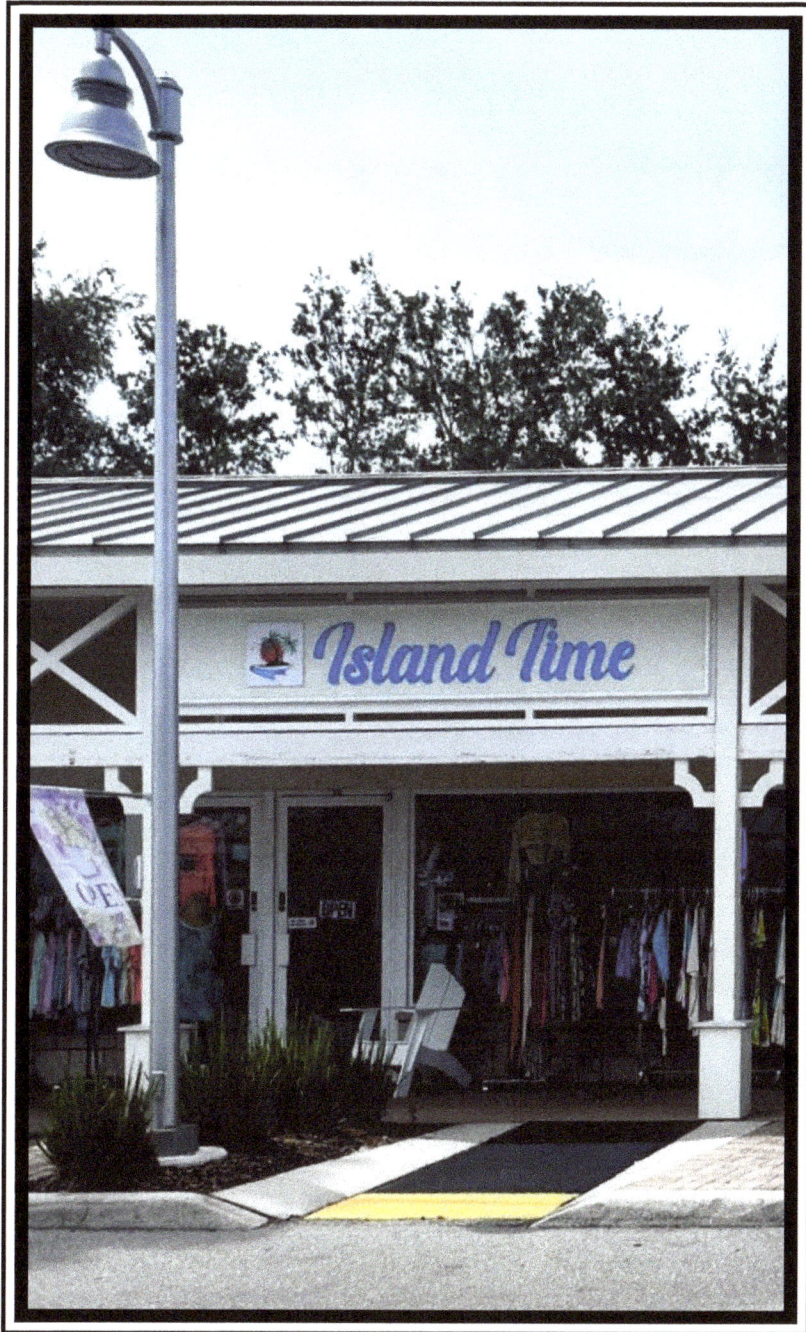

The second time we tried to catch the owl, it flew across the parking lot into **Island Time**, the shop across the way!

The curious crowd at **The Crazy Flamingo** laughed as I ran across the parking lot with a phone to each ear, telling Brittany and Sharon that the owl had flown into the store.

Brittany and Sharon told me they were on their way.

While Fran apologized to the ladies in Island Time for chasing the owl into their shop, I tried to call the owl to come down.

The owl was too wise to get caught. It just stood still and stared down at me from a T-shirt hanging high up by the ceiling.

We told the ladies in Island Time that help was on the way.

I returned Fran's phone, she went back to work, and I went back to dinner.

Sharon was closest to Island Time. She arrived first. Brittany was quick to follow.

After dinner, I went to see Fran. We texted Brittany and Sharon to ask how the owl was doing.

Brittany said that she and Sharon worked together to net the owl and take it to the Conservancy for care. Its behavior seemed suspicious of rodent poisoning.

Brittany thanked us for reporting that the owl was in danger. She assured us that the owl would receive the best of care.

Weeks later, I anxiously texted Brittany and Sharon and asked them for an update.

Brittany quickly texted back...

... with **happy news**!

The owl recovered and was released to the wild!

When I shared the wonderful news with Fran, she was thrilled to learn that the owl had been saved!

Thanks to our texts, our calls, and the expert care of Marco Island Owl Watch and Audubon Western Everglades...

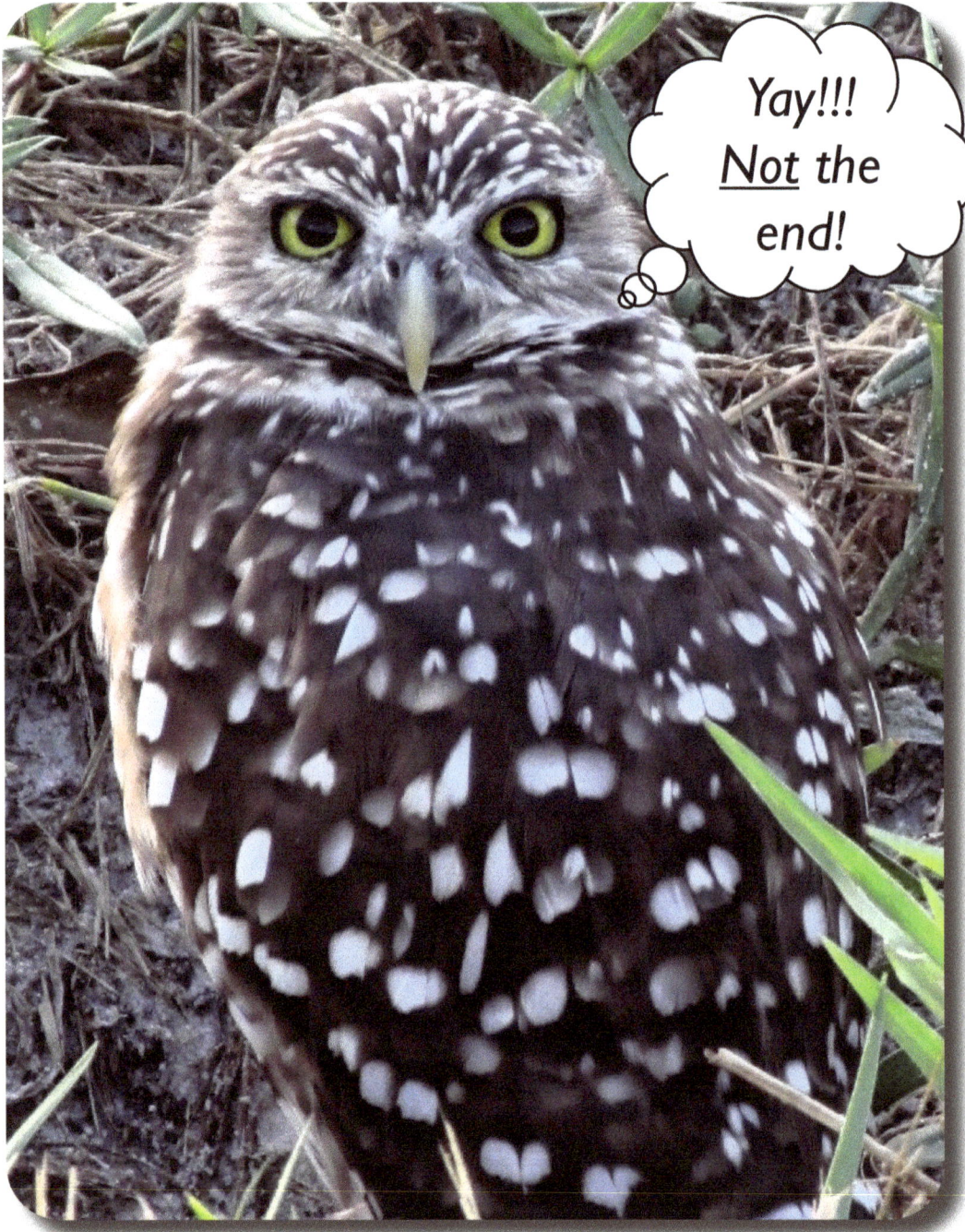

Our lucky little owl lived happily ever after!

Please help our owls safely do their job.

Marco Island's awesome Owl Watch volunteers are committed to raising public awareness of the severe impacts of rat poison on our burrowing owls.

Our sweet little owls help control the pest population by eating rats, mice and other rodents. But when an owl eats a poisoned rodent, the owl gets poisoned, too.

To learn about safe alternatives to any type of poison, please email:

owlwatchmarco@gmail.com

www.ingramcontent.com/pod-product-compliance
Lightning Source LLC
Chambersburg PA
CBHW041600260326
41914CB00011B/1331

About the Author

Melissa Waters grew up in upstate New York and retired from a career in human resources management with the State of New York in New York City. She now gratefully enjoys life in Marco Island, Florida, especially exploring the beautiful crescent beach and observing island wildlife.